QUESADILLA COOKERY

QUESADILLA RECIPES COOKBOOK

First Printing: 2017

ISBN-13: 978-1547049578

ISBN-10: 154704957X

Cover Photo Credit "Fado Irish Pub Chicken Boxty Quesadilla Happy Hour" by *Fado Irish Pub* is licensed under CC BY 2.0

CONTENTS

INTRODUCTION

"Chicken Quesadillas @ Fegley's Burrito Works" by _Lehigh Valley, PA_ is licensed under CC BY 2.0

Translated into English, quesadilla means "little cheesy thing", and boy, are they ever! A quesadilla is a very simple concept: two tortillas toasted in a pan, stuffed with cheese and a variety of fillings. Although the concept of a real authentic quesadilla varies depending on where you are (and what chef you're talking to), there are literally an endless variety of fillings that give you a delicious result!

The basic concept is simple, but you can riff on it endlessly: use any combo of leftover veggies and meat from the refrigerator to feed a horde of hungry kids, or head out to the store to buy special ingredients for something truly delightful for a cocktail party. However you decide to do it, a quesadilla is sure to please everybody around the table.

As you'll see in the following recipes, the only limit is your imagination! Any flavors you like can work in a quesadilla; sweet, savory, whatever! I'd suggest using enough cheese to hold everything together, and keeping the fillings on the lighter side (about half a cup per quesadilla) so they will hold together nicely.

"Tips and Tricks" by *Owen Moore* is licensed under CC BY 2.0

Some tricks I've learned are to pay close attention to your temperature- every stove burner is different (you'll have to see where you like it for maximum crispiness without burning! I've found that I really prefer the larger flour tortillas, but some people love the more traditional corn tortillas. Try them both and see what you like! I also have found that where oil and butter is concerned, less is more! For some reason, the tortillas crisp better in a hot pan with less oil.

Although tacos are traditionally made with corn tortillas, I really prefer the stretchiness and flexibility that comes with a flour tortilla (and they come in bigger sizes!). This will help both with cutting them and also flipping them. While we're talking about flipping quesadillas, I'm going to advocate for making them in a half moon shape (one tortilla folded in half over the fillings) rather than the stacked method, where one tortilla is on the bottom, with the fillings in the middle and another tortilla on the top. This will make flipping infinitely easier, trust me! That being said, many of the recipes in this book call for the stacked method, which can make for a delicious quesadilla as well, it's just a little thicker. With a little practice, you'll become a master of both methods!

I'm going to strongly suggest that you prep all your fillings ahead of time, so that once you get cooking, it's all ready to go. Also make sure that you aren't using too much filling, as that will also make it hard to flip. Heat your pan with a little neutral flavored oil (like canola oil, or a lighter colored olive oil). Put your tortilla in the pan, spread with fillings, and then fold it in half. When the time comes for flipping, simply ease a spatula under the open side of the tortilla, and flip toward the fold. Typically, it takes about a minute to a minute and a half on each side to get nice and crispy, but this varies depending on your pan and your stove! Let your eyes and nose be your guide. Happy cooking!

One final note... if you absolutely must, you can reheat a quesadilla in the oven on 350, but they will never be as good as they are fresh and toasty straight out of the pan!

"Pico de Gallo" by *Hungry Dudes* is licensed under CC BY 2.0

This is a classic flour quesadilla, stuffed to the brim with sliced chicken and a blend of fresh pico de gallo, onion and pepper, and bursting with Monterey Jack cheese. The fresh pico de gallo is not to be missed- it ties the whole recipe together! Try to hunt down fresh cilantro and ripe tomatoes- you'll thank me later!

Ingredients:

- 2 tomatoes, diced
- 1 onion, finely chopped
- 2 limes, juiced
- 2 tablespoons chopped fresh cilantro
- 1 jalapeno pepper, seeded and minced
- salt and pepper to taste
- 2 tablespoons olive oil, divided
- 2 skinless, boneless chicken breast halves; cut into strips

- 1/2 onion, thinly sliced
- 1 green bell pepper, thinly sliced
- 2 cloves garlic, minced
- 4 (12 inch) flour tortillas
- 1 cup shredded Monterey Jack cheese
- 1/4 cup sour cream, for topping

Directions:

1. Mix together onion, fresh lime juice, cilantro, salt, pepper, and tomatoes in a bowl. Stir till combined, and set aside.
2. In your pan, heat 1 tablespoon of oil or butter. Sauté chicken until fully cooked. Set aside in a bowl, return the pan to the burner.
3. Heat the remaining tablespoon of oil or butter in the pan. Cook green pepper and onion until slightly translucent and fragrant. Add garlic, and cook until well combined. Add in half of the pico de gallo and chicken, mix well.
4. In another skillet, heat a flour tortilla, and add a quarter cup of cheese, spread out over the whole tortilla. Add half of your chicken and pico de gallo mixture. Add more cheese. You can add another quesadilla to the top for a layered style, or simple fold in half for the half moon method. When both sides are grilled to your liking, take off heat, let cool slightly, and cut in halves or fourths. Serve with sour cream and remaining pico de gallo.
5. Continue to make as many as you like with remaining ingredients! Enjoy!

"Jicama, Black Bean & Roasted Corn salsa
(#0385)" by *regan76* is licensed under CC BY 2.0

If you're looking for a way to please the vegetarians in your life, this is the recipe for you! It's a little spicy, very cheesy, and the corn gives it a slight sweet edge. Delicious! This is a great one to add in any leftover veggies you might have lying around.

Ingredients:

- 2 teaspoons olive oil
- 3 tablespoons finely chopped onion
- 1 (15.5 ounce) can black beans, drained and rinsed
- 1 (10 ounce) can whole kernel corn, drained
- 1 tablespoon brown sugar
- 1/4 cup salsa
- 1/4 teaspoon red pepper flakes
- 2 tablespoons butter, divided

- 8 (8 inch) flour tortillas
- 1 1/2 cups shredded Monterey Jack cheese, divided

Directions:

1. Add your oil to a large saucepan, and heat it on medium. Cook the onion until it is slightly translucent and soft. Add the corn and beans. Sit until combined. Now add the pepper flakes, the sugar, and the salsa. Stir until all ingredients are well combined and heated.
2. Heat a large skillet over medium heat, add and melt two teaspoons of butter. Warm a tortilla in the pan, spread cheese evenly, then add a few tablespoons of the bean mixture.
3. Set a second tortilla on top, cook until bottom tortilla is golden brown, then flip.
4. Continue until all remaining tortillas and filling has been used. Slice and serve with sour cream, salsa, avocado, or a little of the remaining bean mixture.

"Prairie Chicken" by *Greg Schechter* is licensed under CC BY 2.0

This is a great recipe to adapt for the spice lovers (and non-spice lovers alike) in your life! It's also made in the oven, so it's a great option for anybody looking to avoid the dreaded flip! Just make sure you brush the tortillas with a little touch of olive oil before they are placed in the oven, just to keep them nice and crispy.

Chicken and peppers combine to make a killer filling in this exciting twist on this quesadilla recipe, especially when you add in the cheese! For a spicier mixture, add more red pepper flakes, and for a thicker sauce, let the chicken mixture sit for a few minutes after it's cooked.

For people that really love it "muy caliente" kick, serve with diced chilies and jalapenos.

Ingredients:

- 1 pound skinless, boneless chicken breast, diced
- 1 (1.27 ounce) packet fajita seasoning
- 1 tablespoon vegetable oil
- 2 green bell peppers, chopped
- 2 red bell peppers, chopped 1 onion, chopped
- 10 (10 inch) flour tortillas
- 1 (8 ounce) package shredded Cheddar cheese
- 1 tablespoon bacon bits
- 1 (8 ounce) package shredded Monterey Jack cheese

Directions:

1. Turn on your broiler, and grease a baking sheet with oil.
2. Coat your chicken with the fajita seasoning, and spread evenly on the greased pan.
3. Cook chicken under broiler for about 5 minutes, or until the chicken is no longer pink in the center. Set chicken aside to cool.
4. Adjust your oven to 350 degrees F (175 degrees C).
5. In a large saucepan, heat oil on medium heat. Combine green and red peppers with the onion in the saucepan. Add in chicken. Cook for about ten minutes, until all veggies have softened.
6. Set a tortilla on the baking sheet (don't forget to brush with oil!). Cover half the tortilla with the veggie and chicken mix, then cover completely with Cheddar and Monterey Jack cheese, and then a dash of the bacon bits.
7. Fold the tortillas in half (in the C-Fold method) and continue until all tortillas and mixture have been used.
8. Pop them in the oven and bake until all cheese has melted, probably about 10-15 minutes.

"Vegetarian Chicken" by *Mike Goren* is licensed under CC BY 2.0

These are incredibly useful for using old veggies in your fridge, or trying out new ones! Great for a meal, a snack, or an appetizer for a party. Feel free to add or subtract any veggies that you like (or need to use up!). I love eating these while they are still warm topped with avocado, sour cream, or even a hot or mild salsa.

Ingredients:

- 1/2 cup chopped red bell pepper
- 1/2 cup chopped zucchini
- 1/2 cup chopped yellow squash
- 1/2 cup chopped red onion
- 1/2 cup chopped mushrooms
- 1 tablespoon olive oil
- cooking spray
- 6 (9 inch) whole wheat tortillas
- 1 1/4 cups shredded sharp Cheddar cheese

Directions:

1. Heat a large skillet to medium heat, and add the olive oil. Sauté the onions, zucchini, squash, onion, and mushrooms until fragrant and soft. Put the veggies in a bowl and set aside.
2. Add a little cooking spray to the pan, and warm a tortilla in the pan. Spread a quarter cup of cheese over the tortilla, and then add a little more than half a cup of the veggie mixture over the cheese.
3. Before you add the top tortilla, sprinkle a little more cheese on the very top of the veggies. Cook until golden brown, then flip.
4. Repeat with remaining tortillas and veggie mix. Slice into quarters or eighths and serve salsa and/or guacamole and sour cream. Also delicious with a lime wedge!

This is a great example of how to use leftover meat in a quesadilla, which is exactly how I came up with this recipe! I had leftover steak, and voila: fajita quesadillas! Feel free to adjust the amount of veggies and steak to your personal taste. Top these with salsa, guacamole, and sour cream.

Ingredients:

- 2 tablespoons vegetable oil, divided
- 1/2 onion, sliced
- 1/2 green bell pepper, sliced salt to taste
- 4 flour tortillas
- 1/2 pound cooked steak, cut into
- 1/4-inch thick pieces
- 1 cup shredded Mexican cheese blend

Directions:

1. Heat a large (10 inch) skillet, add in two teaspoons of oil, and then sauté onion and green pepper until fragrant and just softened. Salt to taste, set in bowl, and set aside.
2. With the rest of your oil, brush the bottom of each tortilla with oil, set it in your skillet. Add in half of your steak, onion, and half of your cheese. Top with a second tortilla.
3. Grill quesadilla in the pan until all the cheese gets melty and the tortilla is toasted. Flip, and cook until browned.
4. Remove from the pan, and repeat with remaining ingredients. Slice into wedges.

"Shrimp" by *Didriks* is licensed under CC BY 2.0

These are another riff on a fajita-style quesadilla, but this time with delicious shrimp. For extra spice, add more chili and cumin. These are seriously delicious and can be used for special events, as well as making a normal night feel like a special event!

Ingredients:

- 2 tablespoons vegetable oil
- 1 onion, sliced
- 1 red bell pepper, sliced

- 1 green bell pepper, sliced
- 1 teaspoon salt
- 1 teaspoon ground cumin
- 1 teaspoon chili powder
- 1 pound uncooked medium shrimp, peeled and deveined
- 1 jalapeno pepper, seeded and minced
- 1 lime, juiced
- 1 teaspoon vegetable oil, or as needed
- 6 large flour tortillas
- 3 cups shredded Mexican cheese blend, divided

Directions:

1. In a large skillet, heat two tablespoons of oil on
2. medium to high. Sauté onion with red and green
3. peppers, until the veggies are fragrant and translucent.
4. Stir salt, cumin, and chili powder into onion and bell peppers.
5. Add shrimp into the veggies, and sauté until they are clear and you can't see any more pink in them.
6. Take the shrimp and veggies off the heat, add in lime juice and jalapeno pepper, stir to combine.
7. On medium heat, heat one teaspoon of veggie oil in a large skillet.
8. Warm a tortilla in the pan. Add about one sixth of the shrimp filling to half of the tortilla. Top with about half a cup of Mexican cheese mix, and fold the tortilla in half.
9. Once the tortilla is browned and crispy, flip and brown the other side. All the cheese should be melted by this time. Repeat with remaining tortillas and mix. Slice into quarters or eighths, and top with salsa, fresh lime, or sour cream!

"Halloween" by *Pedro Dias* is licensed under CC BY 2.0

Just to stay in the Halloween spirit, I wanted to use traditional Halloween colors for this quesadilla, and then I realized some of my favorite quesadilla ingredients fit the bill perfectly: black beans, sweet potato, and cheese! If you have time, bake the sweet potatoes ahead of time so they are ready to go whenever you want to make these quesadillas. You can also microwave them until they are soft if you're pressed for time.

Ingredients:

- 2 sweet potatoes, scrubbed
- 6 (10 inch) tomato flavored tortillas
- 2 cups shredded sharp Cheddar cheese, divided
- 1 (15 ounce) can black beans, rinsed and drained, divided
- 1 cup salsa (optional)

Directions:

1. Turn on your oven to 450 degrees F (230 degrees C). Score the potato with a knife.
2. In the oven, bake your potatoes until they are soft. Mash them in a bowl and add salt, pepper, cumin, and garlic powder to taste. Reduce the temperature of your oven to 200 degrees F (95 degrees C).
3. Bake the potatoes in the preheated oven until tender, about 45 minutes. Mash the hot sweet potatoes in a bowl. Reduce oven heat to 200 degrees F (95 degrees C).
4. Warm a tortilla in a skillet over medium heat until it is easily foldable. Flip it, and add about a third of a cup of Cheddar cheese over the whole tortilla, almost to the edge.
5. Let the cheese melt, and add a third of a cup of your potato mix on top of the cheese. Add a couple tablespoons of black beans over the top fold your quesadilla, and cook until toasty, then flip. Repeat until all ingredients are used.
6. Use the warm oven to keep them nice and warm if you want! Serve in wedges topped with salsa.
7. Slice into wedges, and serve in whatever spooky way you desire!

These are sweet-savory-ooey-gooey perfection: caramelized onion, cheese, and plenty of chicken cooked in BBQ sauce. I have served these with chicken tortilla soup and southwestern egg rolls for a perfect casual dinner. In my opinion, the caramelized onions really make it special- they are sweet and soft and tie it all together.

Ingredients:

- 2 tablespoons vegetable oil, divided
- 1 onion, sliced into rings
- 1 tablespoon honey
- 2 skinless, boneless chicken breast halves - cut into strips
- 1/2 cup barbeque sauce
- 1/2 cup shredded sharp Cheddar cheese
- 1/2 cup shredded Monterey Jack cheese
- 8 (10 inch) flour tortillas

Directions:

1. Preheat oven to 350 degrees F (175 degrees C).
2. In your biggest skillet, add one tablespoon of oil over medium to high heat. Add onions and sauté until oil is evenly distributed. Slowly add the honey and sauté until all onions are golden brown and soft.
3. Add the rest of the oil into the skillet. Add chicken, and cook until juices run clear. Add the BBQ sauce and stir until all chicken is coated.
4. On a cutting board or counter or pan, prepare the tortillas: lay four tortillas flat, and layer with chicken, One or two at a time, place layered tortillas on a large baking sheet.
5. On a large baking sheet, place prepared tortillas. You might not be able to fit all four at a time. Bake until the cheese is melted. Let cool slightly, and slice into quarters or eighths.

This is a delicious recipe for a chilly night when you just want something warm and filling. The casserole of the quesadilla world! For a healthier option, you can replace the ground beef with ground turkey, or use low carb tortillas.

Ingredients:

- cooking spray
- 1 pound ground beef
- 1/2 cup chopped onion
- 1 (15 ounce) can tomato sauce
- 1 (15 ounce) can black beans, rinsed and drained
- 1 (14.5 ounce) can diced tomatoes with lime juice and cilantro
- 1 (8.75 ounce) can whole kernel sweet corn, drained
- 1 (4.5 ounce) can chopped green chilies, drained
- 2 teaspoons chili powder
- 1 teaspoon ground cumin
- 1 teaspoon minced garlic
- 1/2 teaspoon dried oregano
- 1/2 teaspoon red pepper flakes
- 6 flour tortillas
- 2 cups shredded Cheddar cheese

Directions:

1. Set your oven to 350 degrees F (175 degrees C). Spray a 13x9-inch baking dish with cooking spray, or coat with vegetable or olive oil. C). Prepare a 13x9-inch baking dish with cooking spray.
2. Set a large skillet on medium-high heat, and add oil. Add onion and beef, and cook until beef is totally browned, about 10 minutes. Pour off any additional grease. Add in the corn, green chilies, diced

tomatoes, tomato, sauce, black beans, lime juice, and cilantro. Stir all together until well combined.

3. Spread about 1/2 cup beef mixture into the bottom of the prepared baking dish; top with 3 tortillas, overlapping as needed. Spread another 1/2 cup beef mixture over the tortillas. Sprinkle 1 cup Cheddar cheese over beef. Finish with layers of remaining tortillas, beef mixture, and Cheddar cheese, respectively.

4. Heat a large skillet over medium-high heat. Cook and stir beef and onion in the hot skillet until beef is completely browned, 5 to 7 minutes; drain and discard grease.

5. Stir tomato sauce, black beans, diced tomatoes with lime juice and cilantro, corn, and chopped green chilies into the ground beef mixture; season with chili powder, cumin, garlic, oregano, and red pepper flakes. Reduce heat to low and cook mixture at a simmer for 5 minutes.

6. Spread about 1/2 cup beef mixture into the bottom of the prepared baking dish; top with 3 tortillas, overlapping as needed. Spread another 1/2 cup beef mixture over the tortillas. Sprinkle 1 cup Cheddar cheese over beef. Finish with layers of remaining tortillas, beef mixture, and Cheddar cheese, respectively.

7. In your baking dish, add about 1/2 cup beef mixture into the bottom. Lay 3 tortillas across the top (they will overlap, which is great!). Add another half cup of beef over the tortilla layer. Spread a whole cup of Cheddar cheese over the beef. Keep layering in this manner until all ingredients are used. Make sure the top layer is cheese so it can brown!

8. Pop in the oven and cook until all cheese is melted. This will be very hot when it comes out, so let it sit for at least five minutes before serving.

This is a variation on a traditional Mexican quesadilla, with an unexpected delicious twist (the cashews!). If you're counting carbs, this is a great way to have a really decadent treat. Feel free to use less oil or cheese if you want!

Ingredients:

- 2 tablespoons Irish-style butter
- 1 tablespoon sesame oil
- 1 pinch garlic powder, or to taste
- salt and ground black pepper to taste
- 5 ounces frozen cooked small shrimp
- 1/3 cup unsalted roasted cashews
- 2 tablespoons chopped green chilies
- 1 low-carbohydrate tortilla, halved
- 1 avocado - peeled, pitted, and sliced
- 2 ounces shredded pepper jack cheese

Directions:

1. Preheat the broiler in your oven, and set the oven rack about six inches away from the heat source.
2. Heat a skillet over medium heat. Add butter and sesame oil, and let butter melt. Add salt, pepper, and garlic powder to oil butter mix. Add in the cashews, shrimp, and green chilies, and stir. Cook for about five minutes, until everything is coated in the mixture.
3. In your baking dish, add all tortilla halves so they are not overlapping. On each tortilla, add half of each avocado. Add half of the shrimp mixture to the top of the avocado. Over the top of the mix, spoon any remaining oil and butter. Finish each with half of the cheese.
4. Broil under the broiler until the tortillas are crispy and the cheese is bubbly and melted.

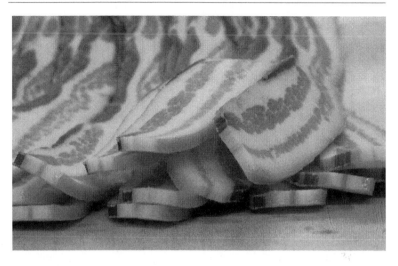

"bacon" by *Southern Foodways Alliance* is licensed under CC BY 2.0

The American South has given us all kinds of delicious cuisine, and this southern twist on a classic Mexican dish is no exception. You can play with the levels of BBQ sauce if you want the other flavors to shine through more, and also with the levels of fresh cilantro. This recipe is delicious as an appetizer, or as a really fun side dish.

Ingredients:

- 2 tablespoons olive oil
- 1/2 large yellow onion, sliced thin
- 6 slices bacon, diced
- 1 tablespoon brown sugar
- 8 (10 inch) flour tortillas
- 1 cup spicy barbeque sauce
- 1/4 cup chopped fresh cilantro
- 2 cups shredded Cheddar cheese

Directions:

1. Over medium heat, add one tablespoon of olive oil to a big skillet. Heat one tablespoon olive oil over medium heat in a large skillet. Cook onion until fragrant and slightly translucent. Stir in bacon and the brown sugar, and sauté until the bacon is well coated and crisp. Remove from the heat and set aside in a small bowl.

2. On one tortilla, evenly distribute one quarter cup of BBQ sauce. Add about a quarter of the bacon and onion mix, about a tablespoon of the cilantro, and one half of the cheese. Place another tortilla on top.

3. In a large skillet, heat one teaspoon of olive oil on medium heat. Cook the quesadillas one at a time in the pan, until crispy and brown on one side. Then flip, and cook until all cheese is melted. Continue until all are cooked, setting finished quesadillas on a plate lined with paper towels. Let cool, and slice into wedges to serve.

If you've ever wondered how to make a Mexican adaptation of a BLT, have I got the recipe for you! The crunchy bacon and fresh basil take it to another world of flavor from many quesadillas. This is a great quick little meal or a lovely side dish. If you'd like, you can cook the bacon first and then use the bacon grease as the oil for the quesadilla in place of the vegetable oil.

Ingredients:

- 8 (8 inch) flour tortillas
- 2 cups shredded Mexican blend cheese
- 1 (10 ounce) can RED GOLD® Petite Diced Tomatoes with Chipotle
- 8 slices bacon, cooked and crumbled
- 1/2 cup chopped fresh basil
- 2 tablespoons vegetable oil Sour cream

Directions:

1. On half of each tortilla, layer the follow ingredients: one quarter cup of the Mexican cheese blend, one tablespoon of bacon, one tablespoon of basil, and two tablespoons of the tomatoes.
2. Fold each tortilla in half.
3. Heat a pan to medium high heat. Add oil (or use the bacon grease!) Set a quesadilla in the pan and cook until one side is browned and the cheese is completely melted, then flip and brown the second side.
4. Slice into wedges, and top with salsa or sour cream.

"Fruits and Veggies and Veggies and..." by *Orin Zebest* is licensed under CC BY 2.0

The perfect marriage of pizza and quesadilla! You probably won't even notice that it's stuffed with veggies. This recipe also used queso fresco, a delicious Mexican cheese. If you haven't tried it before, get ready to fall in love! This is a great recipe for vegetarians, kids, and anybody looking for a tasty way to sneak a bunch of veggies into their diet.

Ingredients:

- 4 (6 inch) flour tortillas
- 2 tablespoons olive oil, divided, or as needed
- 1 onion, thinly sliced
- 1 Poblano chile, diced
- 1 red bell pepper, diced
- 2 cloves garlic, minced
- 1 (15 ounce) can black beans, rinsed and drained

- 1 cup frozen corn, thawed
- 1/4 teaspoon dried oregano salt to taste
- 1/4 cup mild enchilada sauce
- 1 cup shredded Mexican cheese blend
- 1/4 cup sour cream
- 1/2 cup crumbled queso fresco
- 1/4 cup chopped fresh cilantro
- 1 dash hot pepper sauce (optional)

Directions:

1. Brush the tortillas with olive oil, and pock all over with a fork or knife (so they don't expand when you cook them).
2. Set tortillas in an oven preheated to 400 degrees F (200 degrees C) until they are golden and slightly puffy. Remove from oven and let cool on a rack, so they don't get soggy on the bottom.
3. Take the remaining olive oil, and heat it in a big skillet on medium heat. Sauté onion, red pepper, and Poblano chile until they are fragrant and slightly translucent.
4. Place all the tortillas back on the foil-lined baking sheet. Spread a tablespoon of enchilada sauce across every tortilla, and add one quarter cup of the bean and corn mixture. Top with a quarter cup of the cheese.
5. Bake for about five minutes in the oven, until all cheese is melted.
6. Take out your pizzadillas, and top with cilantro, queso fresco, and if you want it spicy, add a little hot sauce!

WILD RICE, CORN, AND BLACK BEAN QUESADILLAS

Here's another great vegetarian recipe! This one is especially filling due to the addition of wild rice. If you like spice, feel free to add jalapenos (pickled or fresh) to the mix. Makes great leftovers! The flavors just get better and better.

Ingredients:

- 1 (8.8 ounce) package UNCLE BEN'S® Ready Rice® Long Grain & Wild
- 1 cup shredded sharp Cheddar cheese
- 1/2 cup reduced-sodium black beans, rinsed and drained
- 1/2 cup frozen sweet corn, thawed
- 2 green onions, chopped
- 4 (10 inch) flour tortillas
- 1/2 cup mild salsa or more (optional)

Directions:

1. Cook the rice- all the directions should be on the package.
2. In a large bowl, combine the cooked rice with the beans, corn, green onions, and shredded cheese.
3. On each tortilla, spread a quarter of the mix. Over the rice mixture, spread two tablespoons of mild salsa, and fold each tortilla in half.
4. On medium high heat, add vegetable oil to a large pan, or spray with cooking spray.
5. Place one folded quesadilla in the pan. Cook until golden brown, then flip. Repeat with all quesadillas.
6. Allow them to cool for a few minutes, then slice into halves or quarters. Serve with avocado, salsa, sour cream, or queso fresco!

This is one of my favorite recipes- very unique and yet all the ingredients work together so well! If you can't find andouille sausage you can try using a polska kielbasa.

Ingredients:

- 1 tablespoon canola oil
- 2 andouille sausage links, finely diced
- 1 Poblano chile, finely diced
- 1/2 red bell pepper, finely diced
- 1/2 large red onion, finely diced
- 1/2 cup frozen corn kernels
- 4 flour tortillas
- 2 cups shredded Colby cheese
- 1 tablespoon canola oil
- 1/4 cup sour cream (optional)
- 1/4 cup salsa (optional)

Directions:

1. In a large skillet, heat one tablespoon of canola oil on medium heat. Mix in the onion, corn, red pepper, Poblano pepper, and one sausage. Sauté all together until all ingredients are soft.
2. On each tortilla, spread one quarter of the sausage mix, topped with one half of a cup of the Colby cheese.
3. Fold each tortilla in half.
4. In large skillet, heat one tablespoon of oil. Set one quesadilla in the pan, and cook for about five minutes, until golden brown and the cheese is melted, then flip. Repeat with all the quesadillas. Serve with fresh cilantro, salsa, and/or sour cream.

Here's a fun twist for people who love the crunchy deliciousness of a quesadilla, but are craving something other than Mexican-style flavors. You can use any mushrooms you like, which can really amp up the flavor! You can also use any onions you like, although my personal recommendation is to use red and purple onions. They have a really sweet flavor that pulls everything together really well.

Ingredients:

- 1 onion, chopped
- 6 large cremini mushrooms, chopped
- 2 large cloves garlic, minced
- salt and ground black pepper to taste
- 2 tablespoons extra-virgin olive oil
- 2 teaspoons balsamic vinegar
- 1/4 cup herbed goat cheese
- 4 teaspoons whipped cream cheese
- 4 flour tortillas
- 1/3 cup shredded mozzarella cheese

Directions:

1. Over medium heat, heat a large skillet and add olive oil. Add mushrooms, garlic, onions, salt, and black pepper, stir. Add balsamic vinegar. Put veggies in bowl and set aside
2. Stir cream cheese and goat cheese together into a bowl until smooth.
3. Over medium heat, warm up a tortilla until pliable, flip it and warm the other side as well.
4. Add one quarter of the cheese mix to the tortilla, spread over half the tortilla. Add one quarter of the

mushroom mix, and cover with a quarter of the mozzarella. Fold tortilla in half.

5. Continue cooking into cheese begins to melt, then flip and cook the other side until golden brown.

6. Continue repeating this process until all ingredients are used.

CINNAMON APPLE QUESADILLAS

Apples are sautéed with cinnamon and maple sugar and then one of the secrets of the quesadilla world is that sweet quesadillas are JUST as delicious as the savory ones. Here's one of my best recipes for a sweet quesadilla, equally as delish for breakfast as it is for desert.

Ingredients:

- 1 Honey crisp apple, diced
- 2 tablespoons light corn syrup
- 1 tablespoon honey
- 1 tablespoon maple syrup
- 1 pinch ground cinnamon, or more to taste
- 1 pinch brown sugar
- 2 11-inch flour tortillas

Directions:

1. In a large skillet, cook apple, honey, corn syrup, maple syrup, brown sugar, and ground cinnamon over medium heat until apples are caramelized. This should take about ten minutes. Make sure you stir constantly so they don't burn. Take apples off heat and stranger to a bowl.
2. Set a tortilla in the skillet, and add apple mixture on top, spread evenly. Add the second tortilla on top. Cook until the tortilla is crispy, then flip. Be careful with this flip, as this is a delicate quesadilla.
3. Top with cream cheese, powdered sugar, cinnamon, or whipped topping.

Here's another fun variation on a traditional quesadilla! Quesadillas take a trip up north for this twist: onions and cheddar cheese baked with steak between tortillas for a crispy delightful savory treat.

Ingredients:

- 1 (1 pound) beef top sirloin, thinly sliced
- 2 small onions, sliced
- 2 green bell peppers, sliced
- 1 cup barbeque sauce
- 8 (10 inch) flour tortillas
- 2 cups shredded Cheddar cheese

Directions:

1. Before you start, preheat your oven to 425 degrees F (220 degrees C).
2. In a skillet on medium heat, brown the beef until all pink is gone. Stir in the bell peppers and the onions, and cook and stir until fragrant and slightly translucent.
3. Add the BBQ sauce to the pan, and let simmer until the sauce thickens and reduces, which should take about ten minutes
4. Spread four of the tortillas on a large baking sheet. Add one quarter of beef mix to each tortilla, and add cheese to the top of each, finishing with a second tortilla.
5. Pop in the oven, and bake for about ten minutes. Flip them carefully, and cook until all cheese is melted and they are crispy and golden brown.

Here's an authentic twist on a veggie quesadilla: add in spicy and savory roasted green chilies and top the whole thing off with homemade pico de gallo! This is a filling Tex-Mex dish that I absolutely love with rice or salad. If you'd like, go ahead and reduce the chilies and spices to make it less spicy or just top it with sour cream to cut the heat!

Ingredients:

- 3 green chile peppers
- Pico de Gallo:
- 1 green bell pepper, halved, divided
- 2 small tomatoes, diced
- 1 small onion, divided
- 3 fresh jalapeno peppers, diced
- 2 tablespoons chopped fresh cilantro
- 2 tablespoons tomato juice
- 1 lime, juiced
- 1 clove garlic, minced
- 1/2 teaspoon salt
- 1/2 teaspoon ground black pepper
- 1/4 teaspoon garlic salt

Filling:

- 3 tablespoons extra-light olive oil, divided
- 2 cooked skinless, boneless chicken breast halves, diced
- 7 mushrooms, sliced
- 1 tablespoon chili powder
- 1/2 teaspoon dried oregano
- 1 pinch garlic salt
- 1 pinch ground black pepper
- 1/3 cup red enchilada sauce, or more to taste

Quesadilla:

- 1/2 cup shredded pepper jack cheese
- 1/2 cup shredded Cheddar cheese
- 4 (10 inch) flour tortillas

Directions:

1. Turn the broiler on in your oven, and set the chilies on a large baking rack about six inches from the broiler.
2. Keep a close eye on them as they roast, turning them one or two times until the skins are charred. This should take approximately 7 minutes, but it's different for every oven! When they are charred, pull them out and (using tongs or an oven mitt) transfer them to a sealable plastic bag. The steam will pull the skin away from the pepper in about 10 minutes. When that happens, open the bag and pull the peppers out, removing any remaining skin. Dice the peppers.
3. Add the peppers to ½ of the bell pepper and ⅔ of the onion, and stir together with tomatoes, jalapeno, tomato juice, lime juice, ¼ garlic salt, ½ teaspoon black pepper, cilantro. When all ingredients are thoroughly combined, cover and refrigerate.
4. Heat a skillet to medium and add oil tablespoon of olive oil. Slice the remaining onion and pepper very thin, stir in cooked chicken and mushrooms until all veggies are fragrant and translucent. Add the roasted green peppers with the chili powder, oregano, a little garlic salt and black pepper to taste, and cook until it's all combined. Add just enough enchilada sauce to cover everything.
5. On one half of each tortilla, evenly spread the cheese, and add veggie mixture over that. Fold each tortilla

in half. Brush the outside of each tortilla with the left-over olive oil.

6. Cook each quesadilla in the hot skillet until they are golden brown and all the cheese is melted. Let cool slightly, then cut into wedges and serve topped with your fresh pico de gallo.

This is a really amazing dish for anybody who loves Gorgonzola cheese, and if you don't- maybe this quesadilla will convince you that you should love it!

Ingredients:

- 2 large skinless, boneless chicken breast halves, cut into bite-size pieces and pounded
- salt and ground black pepper to taste
- 1 tablespoon olive oil, or as needed
- 1/2 onion, chopped
- 2 cloves garlic, minced
- 2 flour tortillas, or more as desired
- 1 (5 ounce) package crumbled Gorgonzola cheese
- 1 cup cooked spinach

Directions:

1. Oil or grease a baking or cookie sheet, and preheat your oven to 350 degrees F (175 degrees C).
2. Heat oil over medium heat in a large skillet. Cook chicken until all pink is gone. Add the onions and garlic to the pan, and sauté until the onion is golden brown and very soft and fragrant. This will probably take about ten to fifteen minutes.
3. Season chicken with salt and pepper. Heat oil in a Set a tortilla on the greased cookie sheet, and layer one half of the Gorgonzola cheese, chicken and spinach, and add the remaining cheese on top.
4. Place 1 tortilla on prepared baking sheet; layer with Pop the quesadilla into the oven, and bake until all cheese is melted. Wait until cooled slightly, and cut into wedges.

This recipe is perfect when you're looking to get lots of veggies in your diet, or you are looking for a quick snack or easy weeknight dinner. It might look like lots of spinach, but it will shrink down considerably when you cook it. Feel free to sub in additional veggies if you have them!

Ingredients:

- 2 (10 inch) whole wheat tortillas
- 3 cups fresh spinach leaves
- 2/3 cup shredded Cheddar cheese
- 1 green onion, chopped
- 1/2 teaspoon garlic powder
- 1/2 teaspoon chili powder

Directions:

1. Heat a large skillet on medium to high heat. Set a tortilla in the skillet, and add half the cheese and evenly distribute it. Top with the spinach, green onion, chili powder, and garlic powder, and add the remaining cheese over the top, then cover with the second tortilla.
2. Let the tortilla cook until it starts to get crispy. Gently flip and cook the other side. Flipping tip- slide the quesadilla onto a plate, cover with another plate of similar size, and flip over, then slide back into the skillet. Cook until browned and crispy.
3. Slide out of the skillet onto a cutting board, and cut into wedges. Serve topped with sour cream or guacamole

I wanted to add a vegan option, both for health reasons, and also to show you how you can get quesadillas to stick together without cheese. I pureed Great Northern beans with nutritional yeast to make a paste that (especially when combined with lots of yummy spices) gives you a Mexican flavored vegan mix that holds your quesadillas together perfectly!

Ingredients:

- 1 (15 ounce) can great Northern beans, drained and rinsed
- 3/4 cup diced tomatoes
- 1 clove garlic
- 1/3 cup nutritional yeast
- 1 teaspoon ground cumin
- 1/4 teaspoon chili powder salt to taste
- 1 pinch cayenne pepper, or to taste
- 1/2 cup black beans, drained and rinsed
- 1/4 cup diced tomatoes
- 1 tablespoon olive oil, or as needed
- 8 whole grain tortillas cooking spray

Directions:

1. In a food processor, blend together ¾ cup of tomatoes, beans, and garlic. When the mix is smooth, add nutritional yeast, cumin, chili powder, red pepper flakes, and salt. Blend until all spices are combined and transfer to a bowl.
2. To the bean mix, add in a quarter cup of tomatoes and the black beans. Stir well.
3. In a skillet, heat the olive oil on medium to high.
4. Set one tortilla in the skillet. Add about a quarter cup of the mix, distributing evenly across the tortilla. Top

with a second tortilla. Cook until all ingredients are warmed through and the tortilla is crispy. Flip, and cook until the second side is crispy.

5. Repeat with remaining ingredients. Slice into quarters, halves, or eighths.

I found this perfect recipe while on a road trip through New Mexico, and thank the sweet cook who parted with the recipe every time I make them. It's the perfect way to get rid of leftover brisket. You can add chopped cabbage or sauerkraut if you like, or using jalapenos, Sriracha, or cilantro.

Ingredients:

- 1/2 cup leftover corned beef brisket, shredded
- 2 (8 inch) flour tortillas
- 1/2 cup shredded Monterey Jack cheese
- 2 tablespoons diced green chilies

Directions:

1. Preheat oven to 350 degrees.
2. Cook onion and beef in a large skillet on medium high heat. Once meat is no longer pink, pour off excess oil, and add in the BBQ sauce. Lower heat and simmer for about five minutes.
3. On a large baking sheet, set two of the tortillas. Spread each tortilla with half of the beef mix, then cover with cheese and half of the onions. Top each with a second tortilla.
4. Pop into the oven and cook until the cheese is melted and they are golden brown, about 10 minutes. Slice into quarters or halves and serve with salsa and sour cream.

This is a true Super Bowl-style quesadilla- a burger, BBQ, and a quesadilla, all in one! And if that wasn't enough... French fried onions and cheese top it all off to make a truly insane quesadilla. Feel free to add extra chilies or jalapenos if you're craving it a little spicier.

Ingredients:

- 1 pound lean ground beef
- 1/2 onion, cut into
- 1-inch pieces
- 1 cup barbeque sauce 4 flour tortillas
- 1 cup shredded Cheddar cheese
- 1 cup French-fried onions

Directions:

1. Preheat oven to 350 degrees.
2. Cook onion and beef in a large skillet on medium high heat. Once meat is no longer pink, pour off excess oil, and add in the BBQ sauce. Lower heat and simmer for about five minutes.
3. On a large baking sheet, set two of the tortillas. Spread each tortilla with half of the beef mix, then cover with cheese and half of the onions. Top each with a second tortilla.
4. Pop into the oven and cook until the cheese is melted and they are golden brown, about 10 minutes. Slice into quarters or halves and serve with salsa and sour cream.

This is my favorite recipe for hors d'oeuvres! It's such a good combination of fun and slightly different flavors. I've added the option of using sun-dried tomato tortillas, which is a fun option for even more flavor!

Ingredients:

- 1 (12 ounce) package smoked andouille chicken sausage, browned, sliced on the bias
- 4 (10 inch) sun-dried tomato wraps or tortillas
- 16 thin slices provolone cheese
- 6 ounces roasted red peppers, drained, sliced
- 1 fresh avocado, thinly sliced
- 2/3 cup grated carrots
- 2/3 cup mild salsa
- 1/2 cup fat-free sour cream

Directions:

1. Coat a 10-inch skillet with cooking spray and warm on medium heat. Preheat the broiler in your oven.
2. Set a tortilla (or wrap) in the skillet, and top with four pieces of cheese. Add half of your Andouille sausage, half the avocado, red pepper, and shredded carrot. Add half the salsa. Then add four more pieces of cheese. Top with a second tortilla or wrap.
3. Cook in pan until the bottom has browned nicely and ingredients are well heated.
4. Spray the top tortilla with cooking spray, and set under preheated broiler. Watch closely, as it will cook really fast! When it's golden brown and crispy, pull out of oven and let rest for a few minutes. Repeat process with second quesadilla.
5. Flip quesadilla by covering with a large plate and carefully turning over after they come out of the oven.

6. Slice into quarters or eighths and serve with a scoop of sour cream.

CARAMELIZED ONION AND JALAPENO QUESADILLAS

I absolutely love caramelized onion, and it really shines in this recipe. Something about the spiciness of the jalapeno and the sweetness of the onion really makes for something special. Sometimes I add meat to this recipe, but in general, I use it as an appetizer or a vegetarian meal. It's really delicious topped with lettuce, salsa, sour cream, and avocado or guacamole.

Ingredients:

- 1 tablespoon butter
- 1 large onion, chopped
- 2 jalapeno peppers, chopped
- 2tablespoons vegetable oil, or as needed
- 4 (10 inch) flour tortillas
- 1 cup shredded Mexican cheese blend

Directions:

1. In a large skillet, melt butter over medium to low heat, and sauté the onion until soft and fragrant.
2. Add one tablespoon of olive oil to the skillet. Set a tortilla in the skillet, and layer a quarter cup Mexican cheese blend, half of the onion and jalapeno, and top it with another quarter cup of the cheese. Top with a second tortilla.
3. Cook until crispy and browned, then flip and cook until the second side is also crispy and the cheese is completely melted.
4. Repeat with remaining tortillas.

CHICKEN, TOMATO, AND SPINACH QUESADILLAS

This is a perfect recipe whenever you have leftover chicken that you need a yummy use for. The spinach and tomato make it very fresh and healthy tasty, and I like to just use the oven so it's even easier.

Ingredients:

- 4 flour tortillas
- 2 cups shredded Cheddar cheese
- 2 cups cooked shredded chicken
- 1 cup fresh spinach
- 1/2 cup chopped cherry tomatoes
- 1 tablespoon vegetable oil, or as needed

Directions:

1. Set your oven to 350 degrees. Set the tortillas on a large baking sheet and spread a half a cup of cheddar cheese on each tortilla.
2. Pop in the oven until the cheese has melted completely. Pull out of the oven and set aside.
3. Set a skillet over medium heat. Add the chicken, spinach, and tomatoes to the skillet and sauté until the spinach has reduced and is wilted. Put an equal amount of chicken and veggies over each tortilla. Fold them in half.
4. Add a tablespoon of oil to the skillet, and heat to medium. Cook each quesadilla until browned and crispy, then flip until they are crispy on the second side. Slice into quarters or halves and serve with sour cream or guacamole.

This is sure to please any young kids in your life! It's perfectly flexible for all kinds of leftovers; you can use it kielbasa, smoked sausage, or turkey or beef hot dogs. I often serve it with baked beans or leftover chili.

Ingredients:

- 1/4 cup condensed bean with bacon soup
- 1 (8 inch) flour tortilla
- 1 turkey hot dog
- 1/4 cup shredded Cheddar cheese

Directions:

1. Pour the soup into a bowl, and wrap the tortilla and hotdog in a lightly moistened towel. Microwave on high until soup is hot and tortilla is hot and flexible.
2. Put the hotdog in the center of the tortilla and sprinkle with cheese. Roll the tortilla around the hotdog. Microwave on high until cheese is fully melted.

If you're in the mood for some fun and unexpected flavors, this recipe is a goldmine! Kids and adults alike love this recipe, and I find I'm making it all the time. If you don't have any honey mustard handy you can always use regular mustard and add a little honey (or even sugar!). Perfect for a sweltering summer day.

Ingredients:

- 1/4 cup honey mustard
- 2 tablespoons pineapple preserves
- 8 (10 inch) flour tortillas
- 1 1/2 cups shredded Swiss cheese
- 2 tablespoons butter
- 2 cups chopped cooked chicken
- 1/2 cup cooked crumbled bacon
- 1 1/2 cups unsweetened pineapple tidbits, drained

Directions:

1. Preheat your oven to 250 degrees (120 C).
2. Combine honey mustard and pineapple preserves. On four tortillas, spread a quarter of the mix, coming to about an inch from the edges.
3. Spread the chicken and bacon over the mix, and top with cheese. Add a second tortilla to the very top. Press down firmly.
4. Using a large skillet, melt a bit of the butter over medium heat. Set one quesadilla in the pan.
5. Cook on each side until golden crispy and the cheese is fully melted.
6. Cut into wedges and serve! Delicious served with fresh pineapple.

This is a great recipe for anybody who loves BBQ but is trying to watch calories (or eat less meat). It's smoky and spicy and sweet, and really flavorful! The secret is finding chipotle chilies in adobo sauce, which you can find at most large supermarkets or any Mexican food store.

Ingredients:

- 1/2 cup prepared barbecue sauce
- 1 tablespoon tomato paste 1 tablespoon cider vinegar
- 1 chipotle chile in adobo sauce minced*
- 1 tablespoon canola oil
- 1 pound Portobello mushroom caps, gills removed, diced
- 1 medium onion, finely diced
- 4 8- to 10-inch whole-wheat tortillas
- 3/4 cup shredded Monterey Jack cheese

- 2 teaspoons canola oil

Directions:

1. In a medium sized bowl, combine the tomato paste, the BBQ sauce, the vinegar, and the chipotle. Mix well.
2. Heat 1 tablespoon oil in a large nonstick skillet over in a large skillet, add one tablespoon of oil and heat over medium heat. Cook the mushrooms for about five minutes, stirring occasionally. Add and sauté the onions, until they begin to brown. Stir veggies into the BBQ sauce mix. Rinse your pan.
3. Set tortillas flat on a cutting board or other work surface. Add three tablespoons of cheese on each tortilla, and top with about a half cup of the BBQ mushroom mix. Fold each tortilla in half, pressing it down gently.
4. Heat your skillet to medium heat, add one teaspoon of oil. Cook a quesadilla until golden brown on one side, then flip and cook the second side until cheese is fully melted.
5. Slice into wedges and serve warm!

The secret ingredient in this quesadilla is scallions- a delicious little onion taste that somehow tastes really special (the bacon doesn't hurt, either!). I like to use this whenever I have leftover bacon from breakfast. A great snack or dinner.

Ingredients:

- 1 pack of flour tortillas; 8 inch
- 1 cup refried beans
- 2 cups shredded Mexican cheese blend
- 1/2 pound bacon, crisply cooked, crumbled
- 2 scallions, chopped Butter, melted
- 1 cup sour cream
- 1 cup chunky salsa

Directions:

1. Lay tortillas flat. Top one half of every tortilla with cheese, beans, bacon, and scallions. Fold the tortilla in half, and press down lightly to make sure they will stay together.
2. Brush each side of every tortilla with melted butter.
3. Heat a skillet to medium heat, and set one tortilla in the pan. Cook until golden brown, then flip and cook second side until cheese is fully melted and second side is golden brown.
4. Slice into quarters, eighths, or halves, and serve with salsa and sour cream.

"Rainbow spinach" by *Alexandra E Rust* is licensed under CC BY 2.0

This recipe is classic, and one of my favorites. Such a great way to get a little veggie boost! Feel free to swap out the spinach for kale or Swiss chard, if that's available to you! Also works well with all kinds of different mushrooms.

Ingredients:

- 1 (10 ounce) package chopped spinach
- 2 cups shredded cheddar cheese
- 2 tablespoons butter
- 2 cloves garlic, sliced
- 2 Portobello mushroom caps, sliced
- 4 (10 inch) flour tortillas
- 1 tablespoon vegetable oil

Directions:

1. Preheat your oven to 350 degrees. Set as many tortillas as will fit on a baking sheet without overlapping. Add one half of a cup of cheese to one side of each tortilla.
2. Cook the spinach according to the directions on the package. Make sure it's drained thoroughly and patted dry with a paper towel at the end, to reduce as much water as possible.
3. Pop the tortillas into the oven and cook until cheese is melted.
4. Heat a skillet to medium heat, add and melt butter. Sauté the mushrooms and garlic for about five minutes, then add the cooked spinach, and keep cooking for another five minutes, until all veggies are soft and well combined. Divide veggies among all the tortillas, setting the veggie mix on top of the cheese. Gentle fold the tortillas in half, pressing gently to make sure they will stay together.
5. Clean your skillet, and heat it to medium heat, and add a little oil. Cook quesadillas one at a time, cooking until golden brown on one side, then flipping and cooking on the second side until golden brown. Cut into halves, quarters, or eighths, and serve with sour cream.

I had to try it eventually; a brunch quesadilla! Eggs are the perfect addiction to this quesadilla to give it a protein pack, and make it breakfast-ready. It's a great way to use up any leftover veggies.

Ingredients:

- 1/2 small onion, chopped
- 1/2 tomato, chopped
- 1 jalapeno pepper, seeded and minced
- 1 sprig fresh cilantro, chopped
- 6 eggs, beaten
- 4 (10 inch) flour tortillas
- 2 cups shredded Cheddar cheese
- 1/4 cup sour cream, for topping
- 1/4 cup guacamole, for topping

Directions:

1. Sauté onion, tomato, jalapeno, and cilantro on high in a large saucepan. .
2. Once the veggies are soft and fragrant, crack all six eggs into the pan. Cook all eggs on one side, flip, and cook the second side. If you prefer scrambled eggs, you could stir them while they cook in the pan.
3. Once the eggs have finished cooking, set aside in a large bowl or plate. Warm the tortillas until they are pliable and warm. Set a tortilla on a plate, and top with egg mixture and shredded cheese.
4. Serve hot! Top with a sprig of cilantro, sour cream, and guacamole.

GRILLED POBLANO PEPPER AND MANGO QUESADILLAS

This is one of my most creative and delectable quesadillas. The cream cheese really cuts the spice, which can really vary from pepper to pepper. If you have a George Foreman grill, this is a great one to try grilling. Something about the flavors lend themselves well to grilling! Unlike lots of the quesadilla recipes listed in this cookbook, this is one where the more stuff you add, the better! The cream cheese really holds it all together.

Ingredients:

- 16 (10 inch) flour tortillas
- 1 (8 ounce) package cream cheese, softened
- 1 mango, peeled and diced
- 1 fresh poblano pepper, seeded and minced
- 1/4 cup butter, melted

Directions:

1. If you are using the grill, preheat it to medium heat. If you're using a skillet, heat to medium.
2. Spread about two tablespoons of cream cheese over half of the tortillas. Sprinkle mango and pepper over the cream cheese, and press a second tortilla firmly over the top.
3. Each quesadilla should be brushed with a little melted butter, both the top and bottom.
4. If you are using the grill, it should take about five minutes on each side to get it golden brown, and a little less time on the stove.
5. Slice into halves, quarters, or eighths and serve warm with sour cream.

Sweet potatoes really are amazing. These quesadillas use mashed sweet potato to help hold the quesadilla together (much like cheese) and also lend a delicious flavor and tons of nutrients. Everybody wins! I use this recipe most often for appetizers, but you could always eat it as a full meal or use it as a side dish.

Ingredients:

- 1 large sweet potato, peeled and diced
- 1 teaspoon chopped fresh cilantro
- 1/4 teaspoon chili powder
- 1/2 teaspoon salt
- 1/4 cup frozen corn
- 1 (19 ounce) can black beans, drained and rinsed
- 8 (8 inch) flour tortillas
- 1 cup shredded Cheddar cheese cooking spray

Directions:

1. Boil sweet potatoes in a large pot of salted water. Bring to a boil, then simmer until very tender. Drain water and put potatoes in a large boil. Mash with a masher (or a fork) and add chili powder, salt, and cilantro to taste.
2. In a microwave safe bowl, microwave corn for about 1-2 minutes, until fully warmed.
3. On one tortilla, spread about a quarter of the mashed sweet potato, then layer about a quarter cup of the black beans and a tablespoon of corn. Cover with a quarter cup of cheese, and top with a second tortilla.
4. Heat a large skillet over medium heat, using cooking spray (feel free to sub out with your oil of choice). Cook one quesadilla until golden brown, then flip and cook second quesadilla.
5. Continue with all ingredients. Slice into halves, quarters, or eighths and serve hot with sour cream, avocado, or salsa.

CREAMY JALAPENO AND PULLED PORK QUESADILLA

This is a delish variation on some fun Mexican flavors. As always, you can add other cooked veggies you might have lying around. This is spicy, creamy, and savory, all at the same time. It's sure to become a real favorite.

Ingredients:

- 4 (8 inch) flour tortillas
- 1/2 cup Jalapeno cream cheese Spread
- 1 (11.5 ounce) package pulled pork
- 1/2 cup frozen corn, thawed
- 1/2 cup chopped red pepper
- 1/2 cup tomatillo salsa

Directions:

1. On one half of each tortilla, spread cream cheese and top with one half of all remaining ingredients, and fold in half.
2. Spray a large skillet with cooking oil spray, and heat on medium. Cook one of the quesadillas for about three minutes, or until golden brown. Flip, and cook second side until golden brown. Cook remaining quesadilla.
3. Slice into wedges, and serve with sour cream or salsa!

This protein-packed, flavorful quesadilla combines so many tasty elements you won't even notice that it can be super healthy due to low fat sour cream and whole wheat tortillas. Comes together in a snap (20 minutes or less) for an easy weeknight dinner!

Ingredients:

- 2 (6 ounce) cans tuna, drained
- 1/2 cup refried black beans
- 1/2 cup low-fat sour cream
- 1/2 cup canned sweet corn, drained
- 2 tablespoons hot buffalo wing sauce
- 1 tablespoon garlic salt
- 1 teaspoon ground cumin
- 1 tablespoon butter, divided (optional)
- 4 (9 inch) tortillas whole-wheat tortillas
- 1/2 cup shredded Mexican cheese blend, divided

Directions:

1. In a bowl, mix the black beans, tuna, and sour cream all together. Add in the buffalo sauce, corn, cumin, and garlic salt. Mix thoroughly.
2. In a large skillet on medium heat, melt one half of the butter. Heat a tortilla in the pan on both sides. Using half the tuna mix, cover half the tortilla. Cover with cheese and top with a second tortilla. Cover with a lid and cook for one minute.
3. Flip and cook the second side of the quesadilla until the cheese is completely melted.
4. Repeat with all remaining ingredients. Slice into quarters, halves, or eighths. Top with sour cream, salsa, or avocado. Enjoy!

THANK YOU

If you have truly found value in our publication please take a minute and <u>rate this book</u>.

We'd be eternally grateful if you left a <u>review</u>. We rely on reviews for our livelihood and it gives us great pleasure to see our work is appreciated.

Made in the USA
Columbia, SC
26 October 2018